Animals That Live in the Forest

Opossums

By JoAnn Early Macken

Reading Consultant: Jeanne
Director, Roberts Wesleyan Colle

WEEKLY REA
PUBLISHIN

Please visit our web site at **www.garethstevens.com**.
For a free catalog describing our list of high-quality books,
call 1-877-542-2595 (USA) or 1-800-387-3178 (Canada).
Our fax: 1-877-542-2596

Library of Congress Cataloging-in-Publication Data

Macken, JoAnn Early, 1953–
      Opossums / by JoAnn Early Macken.
         p. cm. — (Animals that live in the forest)
      Includes bibliographical references and index.
      ISBN-10: 1-4339-2405-6   ISBN-13: 978-1-4339-2405-7 (lib. bdg.)
      ISBN-10: 1-4339-2481-1   ISBN-13: 978-1-4339-2481-1 (soft cover)
      1. Opossums—Juvenile literature. I. Title.
  QL737.M34M34 2010
  599.2'76—dc22
                                                2009001930

This edition first published in 2010 by
Weekly Reader® Books
An Imprint of Gareth Stevens Publishing
1 Reader's Digest Road
Pleasantville, NY 10570-7000 USA

Executive Managing Editor: Lisa M. Herrington
Senior Editor: Barbara Bakowski
Project Management: Spooky Cheetah Press
Cover Designers: Jennifer Ryder-Talbot and Studio Montage
Production: Studio Montage
Library Consultant: Carl Harvey, Library Media Specialist, Noblesville, Indiana

Photo credits: Cover, p. 19 Shutterstock; pp. 1, 9, 13, 15 © Steve Maslowski/Visuals Unlimited;
p. 5 © Gary Meszaros/Visuals Unlimited; pp. 7, 11 © Alan and Sandy Carey; p. 17 © Michael H. Francis;
p. 21 © William Grenfell/Visuals Unlimited

Printed in the United States of America

1 2 3 4 5 6 7 8 9 14 13 12 11 10 09

Table of Contents

Boldface words appear in the glossary.

Baby Opossums

A mother opossum carries her babies in her **pouch**. The pouch is like a pocket. It may hold twelve tiny babies. They have no hair. They cannot see or hear.

babies

The babies drink milk from their mother. After about two months, they open their eyes. They look out at the world. They crawl out of the pouch.

Baby opossums stay near their mother. She shows them how to find food and climb trees. She carries them on her back.

Tiny Climbers

Opossums have long noses with whiskers. Their fur is gray and white.

whiskers

Opossums are good climbers. They hold on to branches with their sharp **claws** and long tails. Babies can even hang by their tails!

claws

Nighttime Hunters

Opossums are **nocturnal** (NAHK-ter-nahl). They are active at night. They hunt for food. They climb trees to escape from danger.

Opossums sniff to find their food. They eat grass and fruit. They also eat eggs, insects, and small animals.

egg

During the day, opossums sleep in **dens**. A den may be in a log or a tree stump. It may be an old den from another animal.

den

An opossum in danger may stay very still. Other animals think it is dead. They leave it alone.

Fast Facts

Length	about 3 feet (1 meter) nose to tail
Weight	about 14 pounds (6 kilograms)
Diet	insects, birds, small animals, grass, eggs, and fruit
Average life span	up to 4 years

Glossary

claws: sharp, curved nails on an animal's foot

dens: places where wild animals rest or live

nocturnal: active mostly at night

pouch: a body part that is like a pocket

For More Information

Books

Opossums. Backyard Animals (series).
Christine Webster (Weigl Publishers, 2007)

Opossums. William J. Ripple (Capstone Press, 2006)

Web Sites

The National Opossum Society
www.opossum.org
Visit this site for lots of interesting facts and fun photos.

Virginia Opossum
www.enchantedlearning.com/subjects/mammals/marsupial/vaopossumprintout.shtml
Find a diagram you can print out and color.

Index

About the Author

JoAnn Early Macken is the author of two rhyming picture books, *Sing-Along Song* and *Cats on Judy*, and more than 80 nonfiction books for children. Her poems have appeared in several children's magazines. She lives in Wisconsin with her husband and their two sons.